Garden Cu...
Tabitha L. Barnett

Copyright ©2017 Tabitha L. Barnett

This publication is protected by copyright law. Please respect the law. No part of this publication can be reproduced, reused, republished, or stored in a database or retrieval system without prior written consent from the artist. The one exception to this policy is that you are premitted to photocopy the original pages in this book to color for your own personal use.

ISBN-13: 978-1975646714
ISBN-10: 1975646711

©2017 Tabitha Barnett   facebook.com/tabbystangledart

©2017 Tabitha Barnett

facebook.com/tabbystangledart

©2017 Tabitha Barnett

facebook.com/tabbystangledart

©2017 Tabitha Barnett facebook.com/tabbystangledart

©2017 Tabitha Barnett

facebook.com/tabbystangledart

©2017 Tabitha Barnett

facebook.com/tabbystangledart

©2017 Tabitha Barnett

facebook.com/tabbystangledart

©2017 Tabitha Barnett

facebook.com/tabbystangledart

©2017 Tabitha Barnett

facebook.com/tabbystangledart

©2017 Tabitha Barnett

facebook.com/tabbystangledart

©2017 Tabitha Barnett

facebook.com/tabbystangledart

©2017 Tabitha Barnett

facebook.com/tabbystangledart

©2017 Tabitha Barnett

facebook.com/tabbystangledart

©2017 Tabitha Barnett

faccbook.com/tabbystangledart

©2017 Tabitha Barnett

facebook.com/tabbystangledart

©2017 Tabitha Barnett

facebook.com/tabbystangledart

©2017 Tabitha Barnett

faccbook.com/tabbystangledart

©2017 Tabitha Barnett

facebook.com/tabbystangledart

©2017 Tabitha Barnett

facebook.com/tabbystangledart

Color Test Sheet

Join the conversation on facebook:
vw.facebook.com/tabbystangledart

If you enjoyed this book, please consider taking a few minutes to leave a review on Amazon.

Please post your colored images online with
#tabbystangledart or **#tabbyb** so I can find them easily.

Instagram: @tabbystangledart
Twitter: @tabbyleann
www.patreon.com/tabbyb
www.sellfy.com/tabbyb
www.redbubble.com/people/tabbyb
www.amazon.com/author/tabbystangledart
http://tinyurl.com/tabbytube

Made in the USA
Las Vegas, NV
23 December 2024